VIRGINIA WOOLF IN 90 MINUTES

Virginia Woolf
IN 90 MINUTES

Paul Strathern

IVAN R. DEE
CHICAGO

www.ivanrdee.com

Library of Congress Cataloging-in-Publication Data:
Strathern, Paul, 1940–
    Virginia Woolf in 90 minutes / Paul Strathern.
      p. cm.
    Includes bibliographical references and index.
    ISBN 1-56663-651-5 (cloth : alk. paper) —
    ISBN 1-56663-650-7 (pbk. : alk. paper)
    1. Woolf, Virginia, 1882–1941. 2. Novelists, English—
20th century—Biography. I. Title: Virginia Woolf in ninety
minutes. II. Title.
PR6045.O72Z8787 2005
823'.912—dc22
                                                    2005007820

Contents

VIRGINIA WOOLF IN 90 MINUTES

Introduction

Throughout her life, Virginia Woolf was drawn to the sea. Images of the seaside pervaded her childhood, where her second home was on the Cornish coast of England at St. Ives. Her novels—especially *The Voyage Out*, *To the Lighthouse*, and *The Waves*—were filled with images of water and the sea. This imagery would continue to haunt her to the very end of her life. In the last pages of her final, posthumously published novel *Between the Acts*, we find a character gazing at a lily pond:

> . . . something moved in the water; her favourite fantail. The golden orfe followed. Then she had a glimse of silver—the great carp himself. . . .

"Ourselves," she murmured. And retrieving some glint of faith from the grey waters, hopefully, without much help from reason, she followed the fish.

Later, at a moment of crisis, we find:

From the earth green waters seemed to rise over her. She took her voyage away from the shore, and, raising her hand, fumbled for the latch of the iron entrance gate.

Early in 1941, Virginia Woolf finally completed *Between the Acts* while she was living at Rodmell, her country home just a couple of miles from the Sussex coast. The supreme creative effort that this required had left her drained. Her mental equilibrium, never good at the best of times, was left precarious.

By now she was in her early fifties and had already suffered a series of serious breakdowns, which had involved at least three suicide attempts. The Second World War had begun two years earlier, and by now the Nazis had already overrun France and most of the Continental mainland. Only Britain still held out, with the invading armies gathering twenty-two miles across the water. In preparation for an invasion, the Germans had already launched the Blitz with its concentrated bombing of London. Virginia Woolf's house had received a direct hit, and she was now living permanently at Rodmell, where the entire coast was on invasion alert.

If the Nazi invasion took place, she had no illusions as to her fate. Her husband Leonard, who had loyally supported her through all her travails, was Jewish, and thus liable to be sent to a concentration camp. As a mental patient, she too would face a similar prospect.

Virginia Woolf and her Bloomsbury Group friends prided themselves on their personal frankness and honesty toward one another. This was part of their credo: the open life. Her sister Vanessa Bell wrote her a well-intentioned letter in which she made it clear that she knew Virginia was on the brink of another mental collapse, but she implored her, "you must not go and get ill just now. . . . You don't know how much I depend on you. Do please be sensible for that if for no other reason." Around this time Virginia made contact with her publisher John Lehmann, who together with her husband Leonard now ran the Hogarth Press. She gave him the manuscript of *Between the Acts* but told him that in her opinion it was a failure: "Its [sic] much too slight and sketchy." Lehmann disagreed with her verdict, and without informing her went ahead with plans for publication, placing an advertisement for the forthcoming novel in a magazine.

In the ensuing days, Virginia Woolf's mental health began to deteriorate. As in previous attacks, she began hearing voices. She became certain that she was going mad. She wrote a letter to her sister, which she did not post, saying: "I have fought against it, but I cant any longer." Early on the morning of March 28 she wrote a letter to her husband, beginning: "Dearest, I want to tell you that you have given me complete happiness. No one could have done more than you have done. Please believe that. . . ."

Afterward Virginia Woolf let herself out of the house and walked across the field down to the banks of the river Ouse. Owing to the spring

10

rains, the river was running high. She picked up a large heavy stone from the bank and placed it in the pocket of her coat. Then she jumped into the cold, fast-flowing waters of the river. Three weeks later her dead body was discovered downstream toward the sea.

Virginia Woolf was just fifty-three years old when she died. The miracle was that she had lasted so long. The previous decades had been a constant battle against mental illness, with her lucid periods haunted by the prospect of its return. During these lucid periods, by sheer strength of will and at great mental cost, she had managed to produce some of the finest literary works of the early twentieth century.

Virginia Woolf's Life and Works

Virginia Woolf was born Virginia Stephen in London on January 25, 1882. A sensitive child, she grew up in a large house in upper-class Kensington, surrounded by a numerous but disparate family and servants. Her father, Leslie Stephen, had been editor of the prestigous *Cornhill Magazine*, where he had been responsible for serializing novels by the likes of Henry James and Thomas Hardy. Throughout Virginia's childhood he was engaged in the mammoth task of compiling the *Dictionary of National Biography*, the classic reference work. This entailed hiring more than 650 contributors to write entries filling 26 volumes (which eventually included more than 350 entries by himself). Overwork was exacerbated by an inherent tendency to neurotic instability. This meant that the family house was permeated by emotional tension which flared into occasional scenes between Leslie Stephen and his long-suffering wife Julia, a woman of beauty and artistic sensibility.

The household also included two older half-brothers, Gerald and George, and a half-sister, the children of Julia's earlier marriage, as well as Laura, a daughter from Leslie's earlier marriage. As Laura grew up it would become apparent that she was mentally defective. The boys, Gerald and George Duckworth, were on the other hand self-confident, intelligent, and philistine in the conventional British manner. Besides these half-siblings, Virginia also grew up with two brothers and two sisters, three of whom were older than she. Three of these would also exhibit symptoms of mild manic-depressive instability. With such a family, the mother had little time for lavishing emotion upon any particular individual.

Virginia was not sent to school and was largely educated by her father, presumably when he could find the time. His professed belief in a rational approach to life was accompanied by a no-nonsense dislike of religion which was unusual during the high Victorian era of bourgeois respectability. Virginia explored widely in her father's library, and he would question her searchingly on whatever books she had read. According to Virginia, he advised her "to write in the fewest possible words, as clearly as possible, exactly what one meant—that was his only lesson in the art of writing." Her "lessons" from her father consisted of perceptive questioning about the books she had read, and encouragement to express the truth about what they had meant to her. Although she would later say that her father gave her "a twist of the head," adding that "I shouldn't have been so clever but I would have been more stable without it." And she was clever. Alone in her room she soon progressed beyond Shakespeare and the translation of ancient Greek, reading widely in history, literature, and philosophy. By the age of fifteen she was reading Carlyle and attempting to learn German.

But this childhood also had its more normal side. There were daily walks in nearby Kensington Gardens and Hyde Park. Through the summer the family lived in their house by the seaside at St. Ives in remote Cornwall, with the children all learning to swim and playing for hours among the rock pools on the beach. From an early age, all the siblings grew used to entertaining one another with communal bedtime stories. It soon became clear that Virginia's were the most enthralling and amusing, and in no time she was telling a new story every night. From the age of seven she began writing these stories down in a family "newspaper," *The Hyde Park Garden News*, which reported all manner of family happenings and gossip. In later life Virginia would recall how even at this age she felt a "concern for the art of writing" which she had "been absorbing ever since I was a little creature, scribbling a story." She was constantly aware that the family newspaper was perused by the professional eye of her father. As Virginia's older sister Vanessa later noted, "I cannot remember a time when Virginia did not mean to be a writer."

Despite growing up amidst such a numerous and close family, Virginia grew into a complex and hypersensitive child. This was at least partly a result of a number of traumatic formative experiences. When she was around seven, her eighteen-year-old half-brother Gerald lifted her onto a ledge where the dishes were placed outside the dining room:

> . . . and as I sat there began to explore my body. I can remember the feel of his hand going under my clothes; going firmly and steadily lower and lower. I remember how I hoped that he would stop; how I stiffened and wriggled as his hand approached my private parts. But it did not stop. His hand explored my private parts too. I remember resenting, disliking it—what is the word for so dumb and mixed a feeling? It must have been strong since I still recall it.

The event served to enforce a sense of shame about her own body, most notably with regard to mirrors. Outside the dining room was a mirror, which seems to have become associated in her mind with Gerald's exploration. Years later she would recall how she felt a sense of shame when anyone caught her looking at herself in the mirror. In her own words, "I must have been ashamed or afraid of my own body." Despite her psychological sensitivity, Virginia was always able to look back and examine her feelings with frankness.

At the age of thirteen she underwent another formative experience. In May 1895 her mother died, giving rise to profound contradictory feelings in Virginia. She seems to have got it into her head that her beloved mother somehow continued to exist as a phantom in the house. She was a loving presence, yet at other times had to be killed or she would kill Virginia. According to the family, Virginia was "mad" throughout the ensuing summer. Although she recovered, she no longer felt the sense of loving certainty that her family had once engendered.

She now began turning to a number of older women friends of the family as a focus for her emotions. Most notable of these was Violet Dickinson, an unmarried intelligent woman who was over six feet tall, plain, and in the habit of behaving in a manly fashion—on occasion greeting people with a hearty slap on the back. Virginia began writing letters to Violet, pouring out her feelings of social gaucheness and her anguished reactions to her father. But these letters were more than the usual outpouring of intense teenage woes to a sympathetic auntie figure. Her letters reveal a surprisingly self-aware young woman, expressing her friendship in open and humorous fashion. She invented for Violet an imaginary husband, and teased her about her so-called respectability. This she contrasted to her own irreligiousness, her frequent ridiculous social mishaps (such as her knickers falling down in public), and her expectation that she would end up having lots of illegitimate children.

Her friendship with Violet Dickinson, which sometimes prompted Virginia to write her as many as three letters a week, in part replaced her former closeness to her family—even her relationship to her favorite sister Vanessa developed scratchy, competitive overtones. But it was her relationship to her father that soon became the most difficult. It seems that he intended Virginia to become his literary heir and take over the editing of the *Dictionary of National Biography*. With this in mind he had guided her education toward biography and history. Despite her evident intellectual brilliance, he refused to let her attend university—while at the same time sending all his sons to Cambridge. As a result, Virginia became filled with resentment toward her father, though much of this appears to have remained repressed.

Then Leslie Stephen became increasingly ill, and as he did so he became more demanding, especially of Virginia. Even when she was younger, her mother had insisted that she accompany her father on his daily walks in the park (mainly to ensure that she herself did not have to fulfill this role). So when Leslie Stephen took to his bed with what had been diagnosed as fatal bowel cancer, the twenty-one-year-old Virginia was the one expected to nurse him. As her father lingered on, her compassion for him was undermined by her surfacing feelings of resentment. Her letters to Violet Dickinson became almost violently emotional: "The waiting is intolerable. . . . I shall do my best to ruin my constitution before I get to this stage, so as to die quicker."

Leslie Stephen finally died in February 1904, and soon after this Virginia had another serious mental breakdown. According to her future brother-in-law and first biographer Quentin Bell (who married her sister Vanessa), Virginia "heard voices urging her to acts of folly." She persuaded herself that this was due to overeating and began to starve herself. Eventually she went to stay with Violet Dickinson at her house in Burnham Beeches, amidst woodlands outside London. Here, as she lay in bed, she was convinced that the birds in the garden outside her window were singing in ancient Greek, and that the rakish King Edward VII was lurking in the bushes uttering all manner of obscenities. Eventually she tried to commit suicide by leaping from the window, but it wasn't high enough off the ground to cause her any serious harm. According to Bell, "All that summer she was mad." It is almost certain that some time before this her other half-brother George began to behave toward her with a suggestive familiarity that may indeed have been the sexual overtures she took them to be.

Edwardian Britain was a heavily male-orientated, class-ridden society, and neither of her half-brothers appear to have found anything particularly remarkable in their behavior toward Virginia. Even she herself did not emphasize these incidents—continuing to behave in a familial fashion toward her half-brothers, mentioning these disturbing incidents only in a letter and an autobiographical memoir, both of which were composed in her last years. Indeed, in her memoir Virginia claimed that Gerald's earlier molesting had merely confirmed a dislike of sexuality that had always been present in her. All this makes it difficult to ascertain the exact psychological nexus that caused Virginia to develop in the way she did. Whatever the genuine etiology, a combination of a damaged genetic inheritance, an emotionally fraught family atmosphere, incidents of molestation, traumatic deaths, and the comfort of understanding older women seems to have left Virginia a sexually frigid young woman with platonic lesbian inclinations, prone to intermittent mental breakdown. What seems most remarkable is that in between these disturbed episodes, her exceptional intellect and her sanity survived, developing in her a lively sensibility and self-possession which is immediately apparent in her chatty letters to her confidants.

> I cant express my feelings about your back. Fate is a brutal sledge hammer missing all the people she might knock on the head, and crashing into the midst of such sensitive and exquisite creatures as my Violet. I wish I could shield you with my gross corpse. . . . [At Cambridge we] went to a divinely beautiful service in Kings Chapel. Nothing comes up to the Church Service in these old Cathedrals; though I dont believe a word of it and never shall.

After the death of their father the younger generation of the Stephen family moved into a house at Gordon Square, across London in

Bloomsbury. Here Virginia began to meet her brother Thoby's university friends who were frequent visitors during the Cambridge vacations. On Thursday evenings regular discussion groups were held, at which the intellectually minded young undergraduates would discuss such topics as the definition of good or the meaning of beauty. Virginia found all this a little too high minded for her tastes but was pleased to be among such lively company, whose members regarded a woman as someone with ideas of her own. Her half-brothers Gerald and George had always maintained a more conventional disregard of women's opinions. One of Thoby's Cambridge friends was an odd young man with a beard, named Lytton Strachey. After having tea at Gordon Square, he wrote to Thoby's Cambridge friend Leonard Woolf, describing Virginia as "rather wonderful, quite witty, full of things to say, and absolutely out of rapport with reality."

In 1906, Thoby organized a family expedition to Greece, which included his younger brother Adrian as well as Vanessa and Virginia.

Violet Dickinson decided to come along as "foster mother," and the group traveled by train and steamer to Athens, venturing out into the countryside on mules to see the ruins. Greece was a backward and remote country at the time, and the trip involved a certain amount of hardship. When they arrived home, Vanessa was stricken with appendicitis, accompanied by severe depression. On top of this, Thoby and Violet Dickinson fell ill with what was diagnosed as malaria. Astonishingly, Virginia remained healthy in mind and body, nursing the sick as best she could, in the course of which she refound her closeness to her sister Vanessa. But she could only watch in horror as the doctors rediagnosed Thoby's ailment as typhoid, from which he died in just four weeks. Stricken with grief, his friend Lytton Strachey passed on the news to his friend Leonard Woolf, who was now working as a colonial administrator in Ceylon (modern Sri Lanka).

Partly under the influence of Strachey and his Cambridge friend, the brilliant young economist John Maynard Keynes, the conversations at Gordon Square now began to lose their high moral tone and became much more free ranging. Strachey was open about his homosexuality and encouraged others to be frank and honest about their feelings—sexual, moral, and aesthetic. Virginia and the recovered Vanessa competed in their willingness to be open about such subjects, being particularly forthright about "copulation" and homosexuality.

Homosexuality was still very much illegal in Britain and regarded with outrage—particularly in light of the Oscar Wilde trial, which had scandalized society just a decade earlier. This was a society that managed to combine hypocrisy with sexual ignorance. Unlike male homosexuality, lesbianism was not illegal—for the simple reason that Queen Victoria, when asked to sign the bill banning homosexuality, had refused to believe that such a thing as lesbianism could even exist. The minister presenting the bill had blanched at the thought of contradicting his redoubtable queen on this difficult topic, let alone explaining the mechanisms of its practice, and as a result lesbianism was not included in the bill outlawing homosexuality.

The scandalous freedom of speech practiced by Virginia and her sister Vanessa would have been scandalous among any but the close-knit group of intellectuals who formed their social circle. Yet what the two sisters said, and what they each did, were very different matters. Vanessa soon married, and Virginia was left to fend for herself amidst this new "openness." She would later recall:

> I was rather adventurous, for those days; that is we were sexually very free . . . but I was always sexually cowardly. . . . My terror of real life always kept me in a nunnery. And much of this talking and adventuring in London alone, sitting up to all hours with young men, and saying whatever came first, was rather petty.

Virginia's openness included an honesty toward herself as well as others. And though she was afraid of sex, she soon began to realize that there was little danger to her among the guests at her Bloomsbury home. Most of Strachey's male friends were more interested in each other. Despite this, Virginia found that she enjoyed defying conventions. She felt liberated by this new attitude of disregard for the stifling upper-class British mores of the period—especially with respect to reticence. Encouraged by Strachey, she became an avid gossip. But this liberation had its more serious aspects. It encouraged her to think for herself, in ways she had never before encountered in her sheltered upbringing. She became determined to examine what she *really* felt.

For some time now, Virginia had been writing book reviews for various papers. It was Violet Dickinson who had encouraged her in this direction, introducing her to an editor friend. Virginia had been asked to provide an essay as an indication of her literary abilities. As she confided to Violet Dickinson:

> I dont think my chances are good. I dont in the least want Mrs L's candid criticism; I want her cheque! I know all about my merits and failings better than she can from the sight of one article, but it would be a great relief to

know that I could make a few pence easily in this way.

The money worries were largely imaginary, but her self-assessment was not. She may not have been confident in her chances, but about her skills she was in no doubt. And this self-assurance in the twenty-two-year-old Virginia was not misplaced. Her writing was soon much in demand. Amazingly, in her very first year she had thirty-five pieces—reviews, essays, articles—accepted. Within a few years she had graduated to reviewing for the *Times Literary Supplement*. Although this was considered the pinnacle of literary reviewing, it had its drawbacks: all reviews in the *TLS* were published anonymously. Even so, this gave her a certain freedom to hone her perceptions. The other drawback was that her work was often cut by editors (who were mostly male), and their insensitivity to everything from felicities of style to the basic meaning of words caused her much irritation. Regardless of such hindrances, she soon began to develop a witty, mature, and perceptive style, descending to supercilious irony only when she felt the books themselves merited such disdain.

> That a very dusty little volume dated 1828 should blossom in all the fairness of a new edition at this prolific season of the twentieth century seems a somewhat impudent defiance of the laws of nature.

Another offering that should have been greeted with dismissive disdain was made to her in 1909 by Lytton Strachey, who proposed marriage to Virginia. Strachey was a highly amusing and intelligent conversationalist, and there was much that endeared this exclusively homosexual man to Virginia. He also confided his literary hopes to her: he was highly ambitious in this respect. So too was Virginia. They soon became carried away with each other, to such an extent that one night Lytton went so far as to suggest that they should get married. Virginia too appears to have been swept off her feet by the momentum of the moment, and she accepted him. Afterward Lytton quickly became appalled at the thought that he might be expected to have sex with a woman, while Virginia became appalled at the thought that she might have to have sex at all. Lytton went so far as to become terrified that his fiancée might kiss him, a thought that does not even appear to have entered Virginia's head. Fortunately the two of them eventually came to their senses (or at least their separate versions of them). In the course of a long and sober conversation, they arrived at what Lytton Strachey referred to as an "éclaircissement"—a bonbon mot, with suggestions of gooey enlightenment.

This event may have appeared superficially farcical. And it certainly provided some spicy gossip among their close circle of friends, who were now becoming known as the Bloomsbury Group. But in fact this was a very characteristic Bloomsbury Group affair. Both Virginia and Lytton were possessed of a depth of self-knowledge and were also aware of each other's difficult pyschology. Lytton's proposal to Virginia in fact represented an attempt at a daring social experiment. Neither wished for, nor was capable of, marriage in any conventional sense. And within a few years both of them would have entered relationships which were remarkably similar to the one they had foreseen with each other. Lytton would remain a practicing homosexual while living with the artist Dora Carrington, who loved him. And, as we shall see, at the same time Virginia would embark upon a fulfilling but sexless marriage to a man of whom she was deeply fond.

By apparently flying in the face of their different psychologies, Virginia and Lytton provoked easy derision, but in the attempt to reconcile themselves to their unconventional inclinations they were also attempting a social experiment of some bravery. The Bloomsbury Group may have been a privileged circle of upper-middle-class writers, artists, and philosophers, but in their progressive social attitudes they were the pioneer spirits for a more liberal and understanding world, one that would not permeate a wider cross section of society for over half a century.

Outside the confines of her group, Virginia remained socially unadventurous and fearful. Despite this she did accept an invitation to take up unpaid teaching work at Morley College, an institute for the education of working men and women, where free classes were offered in the evenings. The principal of the college, the daughter of a bishop, invited Virginia to give lessons on "Composition," but she soon found that the men and women who attended her classes were not particularly interested in learning how to write essays. They were more interested in stories about foreign cities, such as Florence and Athens, which Virginia had visited on her summer holidays. Unsurprisingly, the sensitive Virginia felt awkward in her role as a teacher of working men and women. She was always aware of the seemingly unbridgeable gap between herself and her pupils—one which she was unable to surmount and her pupils were unwilling to break down. Yet paradoxically, when reviewing books, she always felt she was addressing herself to the "common reader," a classless group which was the final arbiter of literary taste. The word "common" here was free of any class connotations. As she would explain in an essay on this subject:

There is a sentence in Dr Johnson's Life of Grey which might well be written up in all those rooms, too humble to be called libraries, yet full of books, where the pursuit of reading is carried on by private people. ". . . I rejoice to concur with the common reader; for by the common sense of readers, uncorrupted by literary prejudices, after all the refinements of subtilty and the dogmatism of learning, must be finally decided all claim to poetical honours."

In 1910 these dichotomies that haunted Virginia's life momentarily found release in what became known as the "Dreadnought Hoax." Her younger brother Adrian and some of his Cambridge pals invited Virginia to take part in a daring masquerade. This required Virginia and three others (all men), to black their faces, don false beards, turbans, and colorful robes, and pass themselves off as the "Emperor of Abyssinia and his entourage." Her brother Adrian and another friend posed as an accompanying Foreign Office official and a Foreign Office interpreter. The group duly presented themselves at Portsmouth and were escorted by senior naval officers on a

34

tour of inspection of the Royal Navy's greatest modern addition to the fleet, HMS *Dreadnought*. As "official interpreter" it was Adrian's task to pass on to the royal group what the naval officers were telling them about the ship. He began by using the little Swahili he knew, but quickly lapsed into vaguely remembered Latin that he had learned from Virgil's *Aeneid*. The "Abyssinians" replied in solemnly uttered gibberish, with Virginia muttering through her beard, "Chuck-a-choi, chuck-a-choi" as she nodded sagely. An invitation to tea, which might have dissolved the paint on their lips, was wisely turned down "on religious grounds"; likewise, the twenty-one-gun salute usually accorded by the Royal Navy to visiting royalty was also modestly declined.

Astonishingly, no one appeared to spot the hoax. A piquant touch was added to the joke when Adrian learned that the august flag commander showing them around was in fact his distant cousin William Fisher, one of his many upper-class relatives who were outraged by the behavior of the Stephens and their friends in the

Bloomsbury Group. When a friend spilled the beans and the newspapers learned of what had happened, they had a field day. The excitement of this escapade, which required considerable daring and mental strength, was all a bit too much for Virginia, who afterward retired to a cottage by the sea at remote Studland in Dorset for a "rest cure."

In the following year Virginia and Adrian took a lease on a house in Brunswick Square, which was also in Bloomsbury. Here several members of the Bloomsbury Group, including Maynard Keynes and his lover, the artist Duncan Grant, rented rooms. When Lytton Strachey's friend Leonard Woolf returned from Ceylon, on leave from his post as a senior colonial administrator, he too rented rooms at 42 Brunswick Square. He was soon assisting Virginia in the task of finding a suitable small house to lease in the Sussex Downs, south of London, for use as a weekend retreat. Leonard found himself falling in love with Virginia, though she was less certain of her feelings toward him. In January 1912 he proposed to her, but she was so disturbed that she brusquely turned him down. Despite this, Leonard resigned from the Colonial Service, thus putting an end to what had been a brilliant career. Then in May, as Leonard remembered years later in his autobiography:

> I had lunch with Virginia in her room and we sat talking afterwards, when suddenly Virginia told me that she loved me and would marry me. It was a wonderful summer afternoon and we felt that we must get away from London for a time. We took the train to Maidenhead and I hired a boat and rowed up the river to Marlow. . . . We both felt that in those ten hours from after lunch . . . we had seemed to drift through a beautiful vivid dream.

Three months later the thirty-one-year-old Leonard and the thirty-year-old Virginia were married. By this time she was already embarked upon her first serious literary work, a novel which was eventually called *The Voyage Out*. It is essentially a conventional novel and betrays some of the awkwardnesses one would expect from a first-time novelist who is attempting to express a sensibility that does not fit easily within the confines of the genre as it was then understood. Amidst the well-observed social scenes, description, and development of characters, we come across passages of intense poetic quality which, despite their confident lyricism, do not fit easily into the work itself. As, for instance, in this passage where she describes a ship that has passed out of sight of land:

> . . . an immense dignity had descended upon her; she was an inhabitant of the great world, which has so few inhabitants, travelling all day across an empty universe, with veils drawn before her and behind . . . infinitely more mysterious, moving by her own power and sustained by her own resources . . . in her vigour and purity she might be likened to all beautiful things, for as a ship she had a life of her own.

The Voyage Out follows Rachel Vinrace as she crosses the Atlantic to South America, accompanied by her father and her aunt, Helen

Ambrose. On arrival they stay in a seaside town at a hotel where there is an English community, and here Rachel encounters Terence Hewet. The virginal Rachel and the aspiring writer Terence are attracted toward each other, though in a somewhat unusual fashion. Their declaration of love succeeds in being both emotionally awkward and highly stylized:

> "We are happy together." He did not seem to be speaking, or she to be hearing.
>
> "Very happy," she answered.
>
> They continued to walk for some time in silence. Their steps unconsciously quickened.
>
> "We love each other," Terence said.
>
> "We love each other," she repeated.

They both have their separate reasons for resisting any deep emotional involvement. Terence wishes to continue writing his novel while Rachel treasures her independent ability to follow the path of her own self-discovery. This latter is rendered with particular subtlety:

> That was the strange thing, that one did not know where one was going, or what one

wanted, and followed blindly, suffering so much in secret, always unprepared and amazed and knowing nothing; but one thing led to another and by degrees something had formed itself out of nothing, and so one reached at last this calm, this quiet, this certainty, and it was this process that people called living.

Perhaps inevitably, Rachel's involvement with Terence ends in unfulfillment and tragedy. There is also a secondary theme which involves Rachel and her aunt Helen, whose mothering devotion increasingly descends into a possessive jealousy. The intensity of a number of the emotional scenes goes beyond the confines of realism, sometimes to the point where one cannot be certain what precisely is happening. Is it fantasy, or charged realism, or simply overreaction? Such passages ring true to the emotional turmoils of Virginia's own experience, but the more normal reader—the "common reader" whose judgment she sought—may sometimes find it difficult to follow her.

All this was painfully reflected in the events of Virginia's real life. During her engagement to Leonard Woolf, she had given indications that she felt no physical attraction for him. On occasion she wrote to him, explaining her true feelings with a frankness that characterized the interpersonal dealings of the Bloomsbury Group: "when you kissed me the other day [I felt] no more than a rock." Predictably, the first night of their honeymoon, which was spent at the house they had found together in the Sussex Downs, was a disaster. When they returned to London, the two of them called on Virginia's sister Vanessa in the hope that she might be able to shed some light on her sister's fear and repugnance of sexuality. (Or, at least, heterosexuality: it would take her some time before she contemplated any other form of sexuality.) Vanessa adopted a normal, matter-of-fact tone, claiming that she could not see what was the problem. She probably thought that marriage to a kind, loving, and understanding man like Leonard was just what Virginia needed, that somehow it would all get sorted out in the end.

But it wasn't. After these first fraught attempts, Leonard and Virginia gave up on sex together. Both appear to have accepted this, after their own fashion. The marriage remained close and supportive despite the insistent and prying gossip of their Bloomsbury Group friends.

Even so, Virginia's mental health now quickly began to deteriorate. By the summer of 1913 she was seriously ill, and during the autumn took an overdose of sleeping pills. This failed attempt at suicide was no mere cry for help, and she was rescued only in the nick of time. For the next few months she could never be left alone; but gradually the moments of stability returned. Yet even in the midst of these she was still capable of writing: "I begin to loathe my kind, principally from looking at their faces on the tube [the London subway]." Such reflective self-hatred remained ever-present and a constant danger.

In 1914 when the First World War broke out in Europe, Virginia barely noticed. In 1915 her half-brother Gerald allowed his publishing company, Duckworth, to go ahead with the publication of *The Voyage Out*, though this only upset her once again. She was hospitalized, refused to see Leonard for months on end, and was violent with her nurses. Then the interludes of calm returned once more.

Leonard had a little money saved from his colonial days, and Virginia had inherited more than enough to live on. They decided to rent a house in the well-appointed suburb of Richmond, on the southwestern outskirts of London. This was partly to distance Virginia from the hothouse of Bloomsbury (though it did not isolate her from it) and partly because of a certain faint anti-Semitism toward Leonard Woolf, who was Jewish. The Bloomsbury Group were enlightened, liberal, and utterly opposed to anti-Semitism in principle, but their upper-class upbringing and obsession with social bitchiness meant that it occasionally colored their gossip nonetheless.

The Woolfs' new residence in Richmond was called Hogarth House. Here they installed a printing press in the basement to launch what became known as the Hogarth Press. At first this was merely a hobby—in part at least, occupational therapy in which Leonard contrived to involve Virginia. Their first production in 1917 was two stories "written and printed by Virginia Woolf and L S Woolf." There was no intention to make this into a commercial venture.

As a result, they had nothing to do with the publication, in the following year, of Lytton Strachey's masterpiece, *Eminent Victorians*. This archetypically Bloomsbury work sought, with iconoclastic wit and panache, to explode the myths surrounding various revered Victorian figures. Its success seems to have spurred Virginia to a rivalry with Strachey, who nevertheless remained a close friend and confidant.

Virginia had by now begun writing her second novel, *Night and Day*. This is another conventional story, with much social observation, attention to character, and development of themes—the major one being the difference between two women. Katherine Hilberry is writing a biography of her famous grandfather, a poet: a dutiful endeavor which oppresses her, distracting her from her love of mathematics and astronomy. By contrast, Mary Datchet is an independent spirit, capable of passionate love, who works for the suffragette movement. The autobiographical element of this work is poignant indeed, as Katherine reflects on the behavior of Mary, becoming aware of an entire region of life that appears to have eluded her. Despite the author's remarkable control over her material (especially in the light of her experience), there remains a sense that the traditional form of the novel is, in turn, somehow controlling her. As with Virginia Woolf's first novel, there are stylistic indications that she wants to say so much more but cannot find the way to do it. Still, throughout the novel she manages to convey complexities of consciousness and subtleties of apprehension:

> When Ralph Denham entered the room and saw Katherine seated with her back to him, he was conscious of a change of the grade of the atmosphere such as a traveller meets with sometimes upon the roads, particularly after sunset, when, without warning, he runs from a clammy chill to a hoard of unspent warmth

in which the sweetness of hay and beanfield is cherished, as if the sun still shone although the moon is up.

These passages, one senses, are the author's true forte. Her originality, and perhaps even her very motive for writing, appear to lie in such evocations rather than in the more conventional structure that contains them.

Night and Day was also published by Duckworth but achieved little success. Its atmosphere was distinctly out of touch with the new postwar reality: to many, the social certainties and cohesiveness of the prewar world had vanished forever. A generation of young men had died in the trenches of Flanders, and in Russia a Bolshevik Revolution had seized power. The shellshocked soldiers returning from "the war to end all wars" had been promised "a land fit for heroes." Instead many found unemployment and hard times.

But this transformation had largely taken place while Virginia was imprisoned within the disturbed confines of her own mind. The miracle was that she had managed to come to terms with any world at all: it was not surpising that the world she evoked was the one in which she had experienced more settled times. But she continued to write, and in doing so now found herself following in the footsteps of her earlier heroine, Rachel Vinrace of *The Voyage Out*, for whom "one thing led to another and and by degrees something had formed itself out of nothing." Her next significant work would be called *Jacob's Room*, and from the outset she decided, "I think the main point is that it should be free."

She managed to achieve this by abandoning the conventional form of the novel. This is the first work of the mature Virginia Woolf. The incipient freedoms that have been noticeable in her previous novels—the lyricism of *The Voyage Out*, the complexities of consciousness in *Night and Day*—now take over much of the subject matter of the novel. *Jacob's Room* attempts to convey, in fluid form, what would normally be the subject of a biography. It is the story of a life. Yet there is no simple "story," where one thing neatly follows another. And at the same time the

47

apparent rigidities of personality and character are dissolved. There is no such thing as a psychologically realized person who occupies center stage. By means of a series of impressionistic scenes, the writer conveys the life around Jacob Flanders. We glean the facts of his life only in fleeting snapshots—his childhood holiday in Cornwall with his mother, growing up and learning Latin in Scarborough, his undergraduate days at Cambridge, his trip to Greece.

The female narrator never quite manages to grasp the identity of her male subject; she is left outside, looking at a masculinity that remains forever beyond her. Gradually we become aware that this exclusion is in many ways what the book is about. Jacob Flanders's eventual death in the war—as presaged throughout by his name—brings home another point. This life is unfulfilled. At the same time the lack of precision at the heart of his character makes this, in its own way, a biography of all the many similar young men who lost their lives in the war. His character is unknown, and indeed unknowable: he is mankind, human nature, individual life itself in

48

all its elusiveness. Yet, at the same time, in a deeply particular autobiographical sense the central character can be seen as Virginia's dead brother Thoby, who is also now nothing more than a shadowy figure:

> . . . why are we yet surprised . . . by a sudden vision that the young man in the chair is of all things in the world the most real, the most solid, the best known to us—why indeed? For the moment after we know nothing of him.

In *Jacob's Room*, Virginia Woolf succeeded in achieving a "disconnected rhapsody," whose aim is to render the novel "inconclusive." Instead of narrative, we have imagistic scenes; instead of an overall picture, we have collage. In one scene, the fearful fifty-year-old Mrs. Norman observes an unknown young man (Jacob) who has just gotten into her railway carriage:

> She read half a column of her newspaper; then stealthily looked over the edge to decide the question of safety by the infallible test of appearance. . . . Taking note of socks (loose),

of tie (shabby), she once more reached his face. She dwelt upon his mouth. The lips were shut. The eyes bent down, since he was reading. All was firm, yet youthful, indifferent, unconscious. . . .

With a little imagination we can all but smell Jacob during this close scrutiny. Yet as the narrator quickly reminds us:

Nobody sees any one as he is, let alone an elderly lady sitting opposite a strange young man in a railway carriage. They see a whole—they see all sorts of things—they see themselves. . . .

The scenes are linked by recurrent images, verbal echoes, similarities, memories, opposites even:

. . . as if humanity were over, and as for men and women, let them go hang—there is no getting over the fact that this desire seizes us pretty often.

The evening air slightly moved the dirty curtains in the hotel window at Olympia.

"I am full of love for everyone," thought Mrs. Wentworth Williams. . . .

The final scenes are linked by images of sunset: "The long windows of Kensington Palace flushed fiery rose as Jacob walked away." In Greece, "the red light was on the columns of the Parthenon. . . ." Then comes the distant sound of gunfire: in Greece, then in England. It is implied that Jacob dies in the gunfire of the war, and finally we see the room where he lived:

> Listless is the air in an empty room, just swelling the curtain; the flowers in the jar shift. One fibre in the wicker arm-chair creaks, though no one sits there.

We follow the movement of the book through its poetry: this is its narrative, which gives the novel's apparent inconsequentiality a perceptible structure.

Jacob's Room was published in October 1922 by the Hogarth Press. Fifteen months later Virginia and Leonard Woolf moved back to Bloomsbury, taking the Hogarth Press with them. Their publishing venture was by now something of a success. From the very beginning it had attracted writing of the highest order, especially works of the new modernism that was beginning to appear. As early as 1918 the Hogarth Press had received the manuscript of James Joyce's *Ulysses*, whose experimental techniques in "stream of consciousness" had greatly impressed Virginia Woolf. Other aspects of the work, however, had repelled her. Despite the apparent liberalism of the Bloomsbury Group, they always retained an element of snobbism. Their upper-middle-class frankness might have been liberating, but that of less exalted classes was liable to be seen as crass or obscene. Such was the case with Joyce, who as an Irishman, a Catholic, and an exile living in poverty in Paris with a former chambermaid, was not the sort of person who was invited to tea in Bloomsbury. For once, Virginia Woolf's exceptional literary taste failed her. To her refined sensibility, the contents of Joyce's work appeared repulsive and pornographic, causing her to liken it to "a queasy undergraduate scratching his pimples." As a result, the Woolfs had rejected *Ulysses*, using the excuse that it was "too long" for them to publish. On the other hand, they compensated for this major blunder by publishing the equally difficult work of T. S. Eliot. There was modernism and modernism, it seemed.

The year 1922 would prove to be the *annus mirabilis* of modernism, with the appearance of such works as Joyce's *Ulysses* (eventually published in Paris), the publication of Wittgenstein's *Tractatus*, and the appearance of Eliot's *The Waste Land*. This latter would first come out in book form in a Hogarth Press edition. In its own way, *Jacob's Room* was also a minor contribution to this great year of modernism. But it was not until her next novel, *Mrs. Dalloway* (1925), that Virginia Woolf achieved the status of a major writer.

Mrs. Dalloway represented in many ways a reversal of the technique Virginia Woolf had used in *Jacob's Room*. Instead of fleeting glimpses of an entire life from the outside, we have a succession of linked interior voices describing the events of a single day, whose passing external time is marked by clocks striking the hours. (The book was originally to be called "The Hours.")

Virginia Woolf's stated aim in *Mrs. Dalloway* reveals the extent of her ambition in this work. "I want to give life & death, sanity & insanity; I want to criticize the social sytem, & to show it at work, at its most intense." The action of the novel takes place in London on a mid-June day in 1923. The Mrs. Dalloway of the title is Clarissa Dalloway, wife of a Conservative member of Parliament, who among other concerns is preparing to give a dinner party that evening at which the prime minister will be present. Virginia was worried that this largely social life might appear "stiff, too glittering and tinselly," so she contrasted it with the tragic life of Septimus Warren Smith, a shell-shocked war veteran who suffers from delusions and increasing derangement. Although Smith is male, and Woolf saw a distinct difference between the male and the female mind, she used his madness as a vehicle for setting down some of her own experience of derangement and mental breakdown.

In many ways these two main characters represent different sides of Woolf herself: the woman whose life is frustrated by the conventions of social life, and the mind that in its extremities defies all conventions of society and gender. In their own separate ways, both these characters are dominated by a patriarchal, authoritarian society. Both wish, again in their own separate ways, to resist this coercion—by medical authority and by male political power. (Not until 1918 had the Irish patriot Constance Markiewicz [née Gore-Booth] become the first female to be elected to the British houses of Parliament, which was also the year that the suffragettes managed at last to gain limited voting power for women in Britain.)

Clarissa is aware that beneath the surface of her social life there is only emptiness, yet she is capable of both lyricism and sadness.

But the indomitable egoism which forever rides down the hosts opposed to it, the river which says on, on, on; even though, it admits, there may be no goal for us whatever, still on, on; this indomitable egoism charged her cheeks with colour, made her look very young, very pink, very bright-eyed as she sat . . . trembling a little. He was in love! Not with her. With some younger woman, of course.

With a similar intense veracity we also see into the delusional mind of Septimus Warren Smith, sitting beside his Italian wife Reiza on a bench in Regent's Park, as she points out to him an airplane skywriting above them:

So, thought Septimus, looking up, they are signalling to me. Not indeed in actual words; that is, he could not read the language yet . . . he looked at the smoke words languishing and melting in the sky and bestowing upon him in their inexhaustible charity and laughing goodness one shape after another of unimaginable beauty. . . . Tears ran down his cheeks.

It was toffee; they were advertising toffee, a nursemaid told Reiza. Together they began to spell t . . . o . . . f . . .

The ending of Smith's life is similarly distracted, as Dr. Holmes rushes up the stairs to get him while Smith prepares to commit suicide:

> There remained only the window, the large Bloomsbury lodging-house window, the tiresome, the troublesome, and rather melodramatic business of opening the window and throwing himself out. . . . (He sat on the sill.) But he would wait to the very last moment. He did not want to die. Life was good. The sun was hot. Only human beings—what did *they* want? Coming down the staircase opposite an old man stopped and stared at him. Holmes was at the door. "I'll give it you!" he cried, and flung himself vigorously, violently down onto Mrs. Filmer's area railings.

Although Virginia Woolf's use of interior monologue owed much to Joyce's pioneering "stream of consciousness" method, she adapted it to her own purposes. We are able to enter into the mind of her characters, but the murkier depths are implied rather than explicitly stated. As a result, we find ourselves imagining our way into the mind of Septimus Warren Smith as he is about to commit suicide, while at the same time we can see from the outside what he is doing.

Virginia Woolf continued writing literary reviews for several papers and magazines but found the restrictions of editorial censorship petty and irksome. (On one occasion she was not even permitted to use the word "lewd.") She wanted to write about literature, and life, as *she* chose to see them. This resulted in the publication of her first book of essays, entitled *The Common Reader*, in 1925. She was always conscious of whom she was writing for, and maintained that if a novelist ignored her readership her art might become overrefined or deformed. Her own fiction could be difficult and was often in danger of losing touch with her notional "common reader," but her essays attempted always to maintain and reinforce this contact. They are readable and address the problems that interested her in a straighforward manner while remaining very much her own work—containing insights and perceptions of which few others would have been capable at this time. And there was no mistaking that she wrote as a woman: upon this point she remained adamant. The titles of these essays indicate their range—from "On Not Learning Greek" to "Joseph Conrad," from "Montaigne" to "Jane Austen." Of particular interest is the essay "The Duchess of Newcastle," evoking a remarkable woman who enlivened the English scene in the early eighteenth century.

> Garish in her dress, eccentric in her habits, chaste in her conduct, coarse in her speech, she succeeded in her lifetime in drawing upon herself the ridicule of the great and the applause of the learned.

This was the woman who wrote provocative plays inverting the plots of Shakespeare to her own ends, who brought up her family with unconventional originality and behaved likewise, being necessarily willful in order to resist the social pressures of the period. "People were censorious; men were jealous of brains in a woman; women suspected intellect in their own sex."

Here was a woman after Virginia Woolf's own heart. With her own growing maturity and success as a writer was coming a confidence in herself and her place in the world. She was a woman, and she wished to develop her sensibility as such. In a male-dominated society, this would require increasing bravery and self-knowledge. Virginia was describing, in the widest possible sense, what it meant to establish oneself as a woman in a male literary tradition that refused to admit that there was an alternative, female literary tradition. Through neglect, supression, scorn, or dismissal, this tradition had not been allowed to develop. And when this was the case, people like the "crazy" Duchess of Newcastle would remain isolated figures— consigned to "eccentricity" (in the usual and the original meaning of the word—outside the center). Such female lives would thus not be built upon, the seriousness of their life and work consigned to oblivion, so that each coming generation of women would be required to go through the same battles. Virginia Woolf's feminism was not yet so explicit as it later became, but there is no mistaking the presence of her embryonic ideas. She refused any blinkered militancy; yet her humanity, compassion, and insight speak the louder for it. Take her conclusions on the Duchess of Newcastle:

> . . . though her philosophies are futile, and her plays intolerable, and her verses mainly dull, the vast bulk of the Duchess is leavened by a vein of authentic fire. One cannot help following the lure of her erratic and lovable personality as it meanders and twinkles through page after page. There is something noble and Quixotic and high-spirited, as well as crack-brained and bird-witted, about her. Her simplicity is so open; her intelligence so active. . . .

As if all this productivity were not enough, Virginia Woolf also began writing a novel in 1925. And between times she continued with her increasingly hectic Bloomsbury social life. The Group were frequent party-givers and spent weekends at one another's second homes in the country—where charades, affairs, pranks, and high-minded discussions were conducted. Virginia's husband Leonard tended to disapprove of so much socializing, which involved a certain amount of girlish flirtatiousness with other women on Virginia's part. Leonard hardly approved of this but was much more concerned about the undermining effects on Virginia's stability. Then, at a party in late summer, Virginia "fainted": it was the beginning of yet another collapse. This time the cause appears to have been as much physical and social as it was psychological. Even so, she was forced to rest for several months, returning to a semblance of normality only in early 1926, when she once again took up writing her novel. The rest had enabled her to recoup her energies, and she was soon in the full flush of creation. This novel was *To the Lighthouse*, her first masterpiece.

It opens with Mrs. Ramsay informing her son James that "if it's fine tomorrow" they will be going on their "expedition" to the lighthouse. James's reaction is conveyed with Proustian psychological acumen:

> Since he belonged, even at the age of six, to that great clan which cannot keep this feeling

separate from that, but must let future prospects, with their joys and sorrows, cloud what is actually at hand . . . James Ramsay, sitting on the floor cutting out pictures from the illustrated catalogue of the Army and Navy Stores, endowed the picture of a refrigerator as his mother spoke with heavenly bliss.

This bliss is at once disturbed by his father's pronouncement that "it won't be fine." James's reaction is filled with the exaggerated violence of the childish mind:

Had there been an axe handy, or a poker, or any weapon that would have gashed a hole in his father's breast and killed him, there and then, James would have seized it.

Virginia Woolf's stated aim in *To the Lighthouse* was "to have father's character complete in it; & mother; & St Ives; & childhood." In this she succeeded, and according to her sister Vanessa the portrait of her mother was accurate beyond "anything I could have conceived possible." Such considerations should neither contribute nor detract from the novel's value as a work of art *as such*, but like any portrait, the accuracy of its portrayal somehow adds to our appreciation of it. Authenticity, or even assumed authenticity, invests the work of art with an added dimension of conviction. (Our appreciation is increased by the assumption that Leonardo's *Mona Lisa* did actually resemble its sitter, and would probably be diminished if we discovered that this was not so.)

In *To the Lighthouse*, the Ramsay family is at their holiday home in "Finlay" in the Scottish Hebrides (which has scenery very similar to that of St. Ives). Mr. Ramsay is a philosopher who has aspired to, but never quite achieved, great intellectual heights. Virginia Woolf conveys this with a characteristically felicitous poetic image. In a subtle echo of her father's work on the alphabetical *Dictionary of National Biography*, she describes Mr. Ramsay's intellectual abilities:

He reached Q. Very few people in the whole of England reach Q. . . . But what after Q? What comes next? After Q there are a number of letters the last of which is scarcely visible to mortal eyes, but glimmers red in the distance. Z is only reached once by one man in a generation.

Despite all his efforts, Mr. Ramsay "would never reach R." Virginia Woolf portrays him—her portrait softened by the years and a modicum of compassionate understanding—as an irascible, self-centered tyrant who dominates and yet depends upon his family, especially his wife. Mrs. Ramsay is the one who maintains the family unity, bestowing affection upon her children when she can, though not without manipulating them in her own way. But behind her motherly façade lurks a deep melancholy. This can give rise to flashes or irritation at her husband's behavior. When he repeats "No going to the lighthouse, James," she reacts strongly but silently. "Odious little man, thought Mrs. Ramsay, why go on saying that?"

Virginia Woolf uses stream of consciousness—more aptly described here as glimpses of interior monologue—to convey her characters. We see them externally going about their business as well as hearing what they are thinking. At the same time their actions are never submerged by any overwhelming needs of the plot. Indeed, there is no overall plot, merely passing stories, often linked by association, poetically recurring images, or fleeting resemblances. As with her earlier works, this too can be seen as a long prose poem. It is also a depiction of family life as well as being an elegy for the bygone age of her childhood.

The Ramsays entertain a number of friends at their holiday home. One of these, Lily Briscoe, is an artist who is in love with Mrs. Ramsay and with all her family. Mrs. Ramsay would have her marry and become "an angel in the house," but Lily values her independence.

The novel is divided into three main sections. In the first of these, entitled "The Window," we see the family and their friends on holiday at Finlay. Mrs. Ramsay cooks a dinner for them all, featuring "boeuf en daube" (a mouthwateringly described beef casserole which she has painstakingly prepared from "a French recipe of my grandmother's"). This is much appreciated by the assembled diners and reckoned to have been a "great triumph." After finishing the dish, the conversation moves on to discuss French history, Shakespeare, poetry, and religion. Watching the fourteen of them seated around the table, Mrs. Ramsay senses that she has created an occasion that is somehow "immune from change."

In contrast, the next section is entitled "Time Passes." Here a flurry of events unfold in dream-like concentration and poetically elongated moments. The house has now been battered by winter storms, the garden overgrown. It is deserted, possibly even up for sale. In a series of brief parentheses we learn the fate of its previous occupants. These events are told prosaically, with a historical literalness that contrasts with the flowing lyrical prose that encompasses them and poetically echoes their contents. Thus we learn that Mrs. Ramsay has died, as has one of her daughters, and one of her sons has been killed in the trenches during the war:

[A shell exploded. Twenty or thirty men were blown up in France, among them Andrew Ramsay, whose death, mercifully, was instantaneous.]

This announcement—for this is how it appears—is preceded by images of "blows of hammers dulled on felt" (the guns), glass trembling "as if a great voice had shrieked so loud in its agony," and the silence of "indifference." After the parenthetic announcement, we learn of those who go "down to the beach and ask of the sea and sky what message they reported." At sea "the silent apparition of an ashen-coloured ship" comes and goes (a passing grey warship).

The final section is entitled "The Lighthouse," and takes place several years later. It opens with Lily Briscoe wondering to herself: "What does it mean then, what can it all mean?" She has returned to the Ramsay home by the sea and is struggling to begin painting again, a task which involves her remembering Mrs. Ramsay. At the same time Mr. Ramsay and his two surviving children set off on a boat trip to the lighthouse. During the course of this trip James's hatred for his father eventually melts when Mr. Ramsay praises his seamanship.

The lighthouse of the title is simply described: "There it loomed up, stark and straight, glaring white and black, and one could see the waves breaking in white splinters liked smashed glass upon the rocks." It is a constant background, a focus of the landscape, and at the same time a symbol of haunting power. Yet as a symbol it remains beyond simple psychological explanation (a phallus, libido), likewise resisting simplistic literary interpretation (illumination, salvation). Some have even claimed to see in it a female symbolism (its caressing beam, its marking of voyage's end and home). When Virginia Woolf's close friend and fellow "Bloomsberry," the artist Roger Fry, confessed himself unable to understand what it meant, she wrote to him by way of explanation: "I meant *nothing* by the lighthouse." She confessed that she was unable to "manage symbolism," which she found she could suggest only in a "vague, generalized way." Her vast reading experience had instilled in her a deep dislike of literal symbolism: "directly I'm told what a thing means, it becomes hateful to me."

When *To the Lighthouse* was published in 1927, it was recognized by several critics as a leading achievement of modernist literature, with Virginia Woolf becoming established as one of Britain's major literary figures. But sales were modest, and she would never become a popular writer. Hearty English philistinism presided even in literary circles, and modernism was for the most part scorned. Readers preferred the likes of Arnold Bennett, who wrote realist chronicles of provincial life in the Potteries, and earned enough to keep a yacht in the south of France. Without her own modest private income, Virginia would not have survived and could not have continued to support the Hogarth Press, which did so much to introduce works of literary value to the public.

As the years passed, Virginia became slightly more assured about her sexuality. By now she had encountered Vita Sackville-West, a striking aristocratic woman who was married to the diplomat Harold Nicolson. Theirs was an open marriage. Her husband conducted covert homosexual affairs while she was more ardent in her "Sapphic" passions (the current term for lesbianism). Yet Vita and Harold retained a strong affection for each other, and maintained a conventional façade—for the sake of his career and their two sons. Virginia's first impression of Vita Sackville-West was not favorable. As she wrote in her diary, Vita was "Not much to my severe taste, florid, moustached, parakeet coloured, with all the supple ease of the aristocracy, but not the wit of the artist." Virginia had always experienced ambivalent feelings toward such patrician figures—making it easier, in this instance, for her to deceive herself. The subtle gradations of the English class system still clung despite social changes in the wake of the First World War. Virginia Woolf and her brilliant friends were merely bohemian upper class, whereas Vita Sackville-West had been brought up in one of the grandest ancestral houses in the land.

It was Vita who broke the ice, telling Virginia how she was fascinated by her brilliant mind and found her delicate beauty immensely desirable. Virginia quickly fell in love but found any physical response difficult. Vita was understanding, and Virginia basked in her tender affection. Gradually she became more responsive to Vita's coded enticements:

> My dear Virginia
> I have been doing something so odd, so queer,—or rather, which though perhaps neither odd nor queer in itself, has filled me with such odd and queer sensations,—that I must write to you; (The thing, by the way, was entirely connected with you, and wild horses won't drag from me what it was.)

After they had finally slept together, Virginia responded in her own coy code:

> I am sitting up in bed: I am very very charming; and Vita is a dear old rough coated sheep dog: or alternatively, hung with grapes, pink with pearls, lustrous, candle-lit. . . . But do not snuff the stinking tallow out of your heart—Virginia, to wit. . . . Ah, but I like being with Vita.

When Vita's husband was appointed British ambassador to Persia, and Virginia learned that

Vita would soon be joining him in Tehran, she was thrown into a turmoil, though in many ways it resolved the situation for her. She could now express her feelings in the way she knew best and felt most at ease—in words. Her letters to Vita in Tehran were filled with love and deep self-searching about her difficulty with its physical aspects.

The child of this affair was Virginia Woolf's novel *Orlando*, a delightful historical rhapsody which she dedicated to Vita. As Virginia herself put it: "I feel the need of an escapade after these serious poetical experimental books whose form is always so closely considered. I want to kick my heels and be off." Which is precisely what she did.

The novel is in the manner of a long, highly charged love letter to Vita, written in the form of a biography of an "androgynous" figure who appears in different historical periods as "a mixture of man and woman, one being upper-most and then the other." We first encounter Orlando as a sixteen-year-old youth in the Eliz-abethan period, living in an ancestral house which closely resembles the historic home in which Vita had grown up. The playful element is apparent from the opening lines:

> He—for there could be no doubt about his sex, though the fashion of the time did something to disguise it—was in the act of slicing at the head of a Moor which swung from the rafters. It was the colour of an old football, and more or less the shape of one, save for the sunken cheeks and a strand or two of coarse, dry hair, like the hair of a coconut.

The "biographer" follows Orlando through his incarnations. During the reign of Charles II he is to be sent as ambassador to Constantinople:

> The King was walking in Whitehall. Nell Gwyn was on his arm. She was pelting him with hazel nuts. 'Twas a thousand pities, that amorous lady sighed, that such a pair of legs should leave the country.
>
> Howbeit, the Fates were hard; she could do no more than toss one kiss over her shoulder before Orlando had sailed.

74

We see him in Constantinople:

> About seven, he would rise, wrap himself in
> a long Turkish cloak, light a cheroot, and
> lean his elbows on the parapet. . . . At this
> hour the mist would lie so thick that the
> domes of Santa Sophia and the rest would
> seem to be afloat. . . .

After being created a duke, he falls into a slum-
brous trance, which lasts for seven days until
some trumpeters sound a blast in his room:

> at which Orlando woke.
> He stretched himself. He rose. He stood
> upright in complete nakedness before us, and
> while the trumpets pealed Truth! Truth!
> Truth! we have no choice left but confess—he
> was a woman.

As the narrator-biographer puts it, "No human being, since the world began, has ever
looked more ravishing. His form combined in
one the strength of a man and a woman's grace."
The book is filled with innuendo and in-jokes. As
it was subtitled "A Biography," the first edition

also included illustrations of Orlando. Three of these are of Vita in fancy dress of the appropriate period. The book finally reaches the early twentieth century, where Orlando falls in love with the poet Marmaduke Bonthrop Shelmerdine. Orlando suspects Marmaduke of being a woman disguised as a man, and Marmaduke likewise suspects Orlando of being a man, but this does not affect their feelings for one another. As the biographer writes:

> . . . the truth is that when we write as a woman, everything is out of place—culminations and perorations; the accent never falls where it does with a man.

Beneath all the loving in-jokes, such passages hint at a more serious theme underlying the narrative. What is the difference between a man and a woman? What does it mean to be a woman? As a man, Orlando has freedom, but as a woman s/he finds him/herself expected to please men, to "be obedient, chaste, scented, and exquisitely apparelled—things which require discipline since they do not come by nature." Set skillfully amidst such determined skittishness, one hardly notices the polemic tone. Amongst all the archness there is much art.

Orlando ends "on the twelfth stroke of midnight" on October 11, 1928. This is in fact the day on which the book was published, possibly the day on which Virginia presented a copy to Vita, who had read none of the work in progress. Before this, Virginia and Vita had been on a holiday in France, their first time away together. In anticipation, Virginia had imagined in mock Orlando-esque tone how they

> might go to moonlight ruins, cafés, dances, plays, junkettings; converse for ever; sleep only while the moon covers herself for an instant with a thin veil; and by day traipse the vinyards.

The reality was to prove not such a lyrical honeymoon—more a period of gentle self-realization for them both. They were surprised at what they found out about each other. They discussed French literature and their husbands as well as arguing about men and women. Vita discovered that "Virginia is curiously feminist." It had not occurred to the aristocratic Vita, who could always behave as she pleased, that someone might feel the need to formulate a political agenda for her freedom. Vita recorded in her diary:

> She dislikes possessiveness and love of domination in men. In fact she dislikes the quality of masculinity. Says that women stimulate her imagination, by their grace & their art of life.

On their return to England, Virginia presented Vita with a copy of *Orlando*. When Vita had completed reading it, she professed to Virginia that she was "dazzled, bewitched, enchanted." To her husband, however, she expressed certain reservations. Leonard Woolf was as understanding as ever about *Orlando* (and about his wife's relationship with its model). Virginia was pleasantly surprised to find him take the book "more seriously" than she had expected. The relationship between Vita and Virginia now entered a more mature phase: they understood that they both, in their very separate ways, had a deep and unbreakable affection for their husbands. This was far from being exclusive but remained a constant bond—the stable background to their less stable affair. Virginia remained physically uncertain yet hesitantly committed; Vita remained fond but soon reverted to her promiscuous habits. Both found they could live with this, and—judging from the openness of their letters—they remained close for many years to come.

By now Virginia Woolf found herself facing the problems of literary fame. Outside her own group she was almost pathologically nervous. Even so, in October 1928 she accepted an invitation to deliver talks at Newnham and Girton, the two women's colleges at Cambridge. Despite her shaking hands, she presented a striking appearance. Her talks, on the other hand, were delivered with some awkwardness, but their content made a powerful effect that was long remembered. Virginia Woolf's two Cambridge talks would eventually be expanded into a book entitled *A Room of One's Own*. This was to be her finest nonfiction work and has since come to be recognized as a formative feminist text. Indeed, her twentieth-century biographer, Hermione Lee, went so far as to claim that it was "probably the most influential piece of nonfiction writing by a woman in this century."

A Room of One's Own is essentially a discussion of the difficulties facing a woman who wants to write. For Virginia Woolf this begins with one basic, unliterary fact: "a woman must have money and a room of her own if she is to write fiction." In dealing with this problem, she admits that she will be leaving "the great problem of the true nature of woman and the true nature of fiction unsolved."

She outlines the obstacles that prevent women from expressing themselves fully and authentically, and taking a rightful place in a literary tradition which has for the most part been defined and shaped by men. Not least of these obstacles is the attitude of male figures and writers toward women. She quotes the eighteenth-century poet Alexander Pope's notorious (and widely held) opinion that, "Most women have no character at all." She questions Samuel Butler's view that "Wise men never say what they think about women" by insisting that "Wise men never say anything else apparently." In mock earnestness she reviews the attitudes of these wise men through the ages on whether women are capable or incapable of education: "Napoleon thought them incapable, Dr Johnson thought the opposite. . . . Goethe honoured them, Mussolini despised them."

A Room of One's Own concentrates on the particular problems that have faced individual writers through the centuries, how they came to terms with them, and how their writing was affected. These writers range from such renowned figures as Jane Austen and Charlotte Brontë to lesser-known writers who in her day were all but forgotten. Included among the latter are the seventeenth-century poet, playwright, and novelist Aphra Behn, who Virginia Woolf claims was the first woman to earn her living from writing. (A year earlier Vita Sackville-West had written a pioneering biography of Aphra Behn.) Another seventeenth-century figure Virginia mentions is the letter writer Dorothy Osborne, who gave a rare glimpse into the authentic intimate and personal thoughts of women, as well as their relationship to men, from an age where such matters had been almost entirely supressed or overlooked. Largely as a result of Virginia Woolf's efforts, these writers would undergo a resurrection, returning them to the attention of women in the twentieth century after a long period of neglect. As she intended, these writers have now become part of a canon of women writers, who have risen from neglected obscurity to take their place in the larger tradition as well as forming a distinct female tradition of their own. Such women writers have become a source of inspiration for many women—not only writers but any involved in the struggle to free themselves and express themselves in their own authentic fashion.

Virginia Woolf saw the novel as the ideal form for women in which to express their creativity, mainly because its form remained fluid. It had not yet become constricted by any stifling tradition that catered predominantly to male needs. For a woman, the novel remained "young enough to be soft in her hands."

Virginia Woolf's boldest stroke in *A Room of One's Own* is purely imaginary: "Let me imagine, since facts are so hard to come by, what would have happened had Shakespeare had a wonderfully gifted sister, called Judith." Her life is sketched in outline:

> She was as adventurous, as imaginative, as agog to see the world as he was. But she was not sent to school. . . . She picked up a book now and then, one of her brother's perhaps, and read a few pages. But then her parents came in and told her to mend the stockings. . . . Perhaps she scribbled some pages up in an apple loft on the sly. . . .

To avoid being browbeaten by her father into marriage with the son of a neighboring wool stapler, Judith runs off to London. Here she is rejected in her attempts to become an actress and finds her life severely restricted with regard to just the experience she requires. "Could she even seek her dinner in a tavern or roam the streets at midnight?" Eventually she is taken in by a sympathetic actor-manager, but becomes pregnant.

83

On finding herself faced with a life devoid of creativity: "who shall measure the heat and violence of the poet's heart when caught and tangled in a woman's body?" She takes her life.

What is the point of this tale of unrelenting woe, whose lineaments must have been repeated so many times in the past? Virginia Woolf's conclusion provokes us to imagine, and discover, a sorrow that is both vaster and more secret: "genius of a sort must have existed among women as it must have existed among the working classes." Her tale of Judith Shakespeare is a parable of enormous human waste, which might well have provoked her brother to exclaim, as he did in another context:

> O ruin'd piece of nature! This great world
> Should so wear out to nought.

Although long in coming, however, redemption was at hand. As Virginia points out:

> . . . towards the end of the eighteenth century a change came about which, if I were rewriting history, I should describe more fully and

84

think of greater importance than the Cru-
sades or the Wars of the Roses. The middle-
class woman began to write.

In the final chapter of *A Room of One's
Own*, Virginia Woolf returns to the problem she
had expressed so poetically in *Orlando*, "an-
drogyny." She points out, contrary to Butler, that
"No age can ever have been so stridently sex-
conscious as our own; those innumerable books
by men about women in the British Museum are
proof of it." As she demonstrated in *Orlando*,
there is no need for the strict classification of exclusively "male" and exclusively "female" qualities. Men and women share many qualities, and
indeed need aspects of each other if they are to
achieve their full humanity. "Perhaps a mind that
is purely masculine cannot create, any more than
a mind that is purely feminine." She cites the
"man-womanly" mind of Shakespeare, yet
warns: "It is fatal for anyone who writes to think
of their sex." She is against women resorting to
polemical literature. Women cannot free themselves from centuries of misogyny by resorting to

its opposite (misandry). Such a course would only be self-defeating. She insists:

> Some collaboration has to take place in the mind between the woman and the man before the art of creation can be accomplished. Some marriage of opposites has to be consummated. . . . There must be freedom and there must be peace.

Virginia Woolf now returned to fiction with *The Waves*, published in 1931. This was her most experimental novel to date, and in many ways her most lyrical. As was her habit, she formulated her aims for her novel in her diary. Her disillusion with the orthodox novel was profound, and formed an antithetical view: "This appalling narrative business of the realist: getting on from lunch to dinner: it is false, unreal, merely conventional. Why admit anything to literature that is not poetry—by which I mean saturated?" In *The Waves*: "I mean to eliminate all waste, deadness, superfluity: to give the moment whole; whatever it includes. Say that the moment is a combination of thought; sensation; the voice of the sea." Writing such a novel was to prove a deeply inspirational as well as an unsettling experience, with "some moments of such intensity and intoxication that I seemed only to stumble after my own voice, or almost, after some sort of speaker (as when I was mad). I was almost afraid, remembering the voices that used to fly ahead." Writing *The Waves* would bring her once more to the brink of breakdown. Her husband Leonard's verdict, on reading the completed version, that this was a masterpiece, undoubtedly did much to bolster her self-belief and avert another mental catastrophe.

The lack of plot and elementary guidance for the reader makes *The Waves* a difficult read. Yet these very same qualities mean that once readers have broken the barrier, so to speak, the world in which they find themselves becomes both intensely involving and as compelling as any straightforward narrative. In *The Waves*, Virginia Woolf takes her stream-of-consciousness method to a new extreme. The novel largely consists of the interior monologues of six characters as they journey from childhood to old age, becoming involved in a series of incidents. There is also a seventh character whose mind we do not enter. He is seen only as an object of the others' consciousness, involving their emotions and ambitions. His early death forms a focus for their fears and anxieties.

In *The Waves*, Virginia Woolf succeeds in conveying both the fluidity and the precariousness of personal identity. On a purely personal level, this was a constant preoccupation. The threat of mental breakdown made her deeply and constantly aware of the fragility of her own personality. Yet such is the mastery of her literary techniques that this aspect of *The Waves* rises far above her particular concerns, to the point where we recognize the universality of this condition. Our psychology is not irrevocably cast in some unbreakable mold, it is capable of being molded into all manner of shapes, and even of shattering. At all moments it exists on different levels, and in different degrees of expansiveness, which can change from moment to moment. In the final long monologue, Bernard (a writer) addresses his last thoughts to an imaginary listener:

"Now to sum up. . . . Now to explain to you the meaning of my life. Since we do not know each other. . . ." Bernard understands that he has no precise identity, either psychological or sexual: "I am not one person, but many people." He comes to realize, "There was no past, no future; merely the moment in its ring of light, and our bodies."

The Waves contains a subtle objective counterbalance to this at times almost claustrophobic subjectivity, in the form of objective lyrical meditations on the sun, the sea, and nature. The novel opens with an intensely poetic evocation of this outer world—a dawn over the sea—while the inner world of human beings is still asleep, though on the point of waking:

> The sun . . . made a blue fingerprint of shadow under the leaf by the bedroom window. The blind stirred slightly, but all within was dim and unsubstantial. The birds sang their blank melody outside.

Such is the prelude to the separate inner voices. Yet as the novel approaches its end, Bernard's monologue gradually appears to melt into a state similar to these objective lyrical passages. His voice draws to a close at the end of the darkest hour of night, with the prospect of another dawn:

> Another general awakening. The stars draw back and are extinguished. The bars deepen themselves between the waves. The film of mist thickens on the fields. A redness gathers on the roses, even on the pale rose that hangs by the bedroom window. A bird chirps. Cottagers light their early candles. . . .

The waves broke on the shore.

Despite Leonard Woolf's championing of *The Waves*, Virginia continued to suffer from depression after its publication. She had become preoccupied with death, and with some reason. Around this period a number of her Bloomsbury friends died, as well as several well-known writers. Her great middlebrow *bête noire*, Arnold Bennett, died suddenly of cholera, and she was also affected by the death of D. H. Lawrence. She had never met Lawrence, felt some distaste for his subject matter, and was incensed by his savagely mocking portrait of Vita Sackville-West in *Women in Love*. Even so, she could not but admire his raw talent and what he was doing with it. She could see that they were both, in their very separate ways, attempting the same thing: to render the novel more intense and poetic.

Over the years Virginia Woolf had somewhat drifted apart from Lytton Strachey, though his infrequent visits to her country retreat at Rodmell in Sussex would quickly rekindle their old intimacy. In a letter to Vita Sackville-West she described how: "Lytton comes. We sit up talking about Queen Elizabeth, sodomy, love, the Antigone, Othello." She always remained slightly jealous of his more public success, which accounted in part for the distance between them, yet she was nonetheless deeply shocked by his unexpected death from stomach cancer in 1932. Strachey had lived for several years in a *ménage à trois*, with his male lover Ralph Partridge and a loving female partner, the artist Dora Carrington. Despite efforts by Virginia Woolf and other Bloomsbury friends,

Carrington committed suicide after Strachey's death, and Partridge would never recover.

In order to get Virginia away from all this, Leonard took her on a tour of Greece in the spring of 1932. They were accompanied by their Bloomsbury friends the artist Roger Fry and his sister Margery Fry. Roger Fry's arrival on the Bloomsbury scene in the early 1910s had proved a formative influence on the group. He was one of the newcomers responsible for the diversion of interest from high-minded philosophy to the more liberated discussion of art and artistic freedom (to which Strachey would contribute his own more louche interests). During her month-long holiday in Greece, Virginia initially found herself plagued by memories of her previous visit, which had resulted in her brother Thoby's death. But Greece also brought her face to face with herself, giving her frail personality occasion for some healthy self-assessment. While she was walking on the Acropolis, "my own ghost met me, the girl of 23, with all her life to come. . . . And how I pitied her." Her admiration for ancient Greece remained unabated, but she couldn't help noting ambivalently about how such ancient sites had managed to survive: "Poverty & war & misery have prevented any obliteration." Elsewhere, she noted:

> The centuries have left no trace. . . . There is . . . nothing between [recent centuries] and 300 BC. . . . If one finds a bay it is deserted; so too with the hills & the valleys; not a villa, not a teashop not a kennel anywhere; no wires, no churches, almost no graveyards.

She found her companions congenial. Roger Fry was by now sixty-six but remained filled with creative and intellectual energy. His sister Margery, whom Virginia privately nicknamed "the Yak," had an equally stimulating and intellectual mind. Yet as principal of Somerville, one of the Cambridge women's colleges, Margery found some of Virginia Woolf's more liberated opinions as disconcerting as she would doubtless have found her nickname.

Later in 1932, the fifty-year-old Virginia Woolf published the second series of *The Common Reader*. As with the earlier volume, this contained essays on an eclectic range of English historical figures—from Jane Austen to Beau Brummell, from Sir Philip Sidney to Thomas Hardy. Again and again she stressed how the interpretation of such figures shifted with the new readers of each ensuing age:

> Each had read differently, with the insight and blindness of his own generation. Our reading will be equally partial. In 1930 we shall miss a great deal that was obvious in 1655; we shall see some things that the eighteenth century ignored. But let us keep up the long succession of readers; let us in our turn bring the insight and blindness of our own generation to bear. . . .

Here is yet another argument for reading the literature of the past. We are told that we should read such works in order to keep our heritage alive, so that it can give depth and self-understanding to our perception of the age in which we ourselves live. But there is more. In reading such works through the eyes of our own age, we in some way change these works—seeing relevances that were missed at the time, missing emphases that were once considered crucial. We now notice that in Jane Austen's preoccupation with the immediate social picture, she saw no reason to draw attention to the larger historical events taking place around her. Her works make no mention of the French Revolution or the Napoleonic Wars, which caused such social and international turbulence during the period in which her novels are set. Similar gaps abound in English literature and thought. The seventeenth-century philosopher John Locke's ideas inspired the notions of individual liberty that appeared in the U.S. Constitution, yet we now discover that he held shares in slave plantations. Even Karl Marx employed a servant and made her pregnant. All this gives us new eyes, makes us more aware. Yet, as Virginia Woolf reminds us, the "blindness of our own generation" may prove as crucial to those of ensuing generations. This we must constantly bear in mind, especially when making our own "definitive" judgments.

As ever, Virginia Woolf has much to say about earlier female literary figures, and not all of it is favorable. She cites *Aurora Leigh*, written by Elizabeth Barrett Browning:

> If . . . we take *Aurora Leigh* from the shelf it is not so much to read it as to muse with kindly condescension over this token of by-gone fashion, as we toy with the fringes of our grandmothers' mantle and muse over the alabaster models of the Taj Mahal which once adorned their drawing room tables. But to the Victorians, undoubtedly, this book was very dear.

Within sixteen years of its publication in 1857, *Aurora Leigh* had gone through no less than thirteen editions, and its author later came to consider it "the most mature of my works." *Aurora Leigh* recounts, semi-autobiographically, a woman's struggles to establish herself as a poet. We only have to mention that this "novel-poem" consists of nine volumes of blank verse for many to consider that they understand why it is no longer regarded as a great popular work. But

Virginia Woolf goes much further, analyzing why the work fails as *poetry*, why the seeds of its undoing lay in the author and her chosen method for its composition. Through long years of solitude she had contemplated writing such a work, and only when she finally achieved her freedom did she actually write it:

> What damage had her life done to her as a poet? A great one, we cannot deny. For it is clear, as we turn the pages of *Aurora Leigh* . . . that the mind which found its natural expression in this swift and chaotic poem about real men and women was not the mind to profit by solitude. A lyrical, a scholarly, a fastidious mind might have used seclusion and solitude to perfect its powers. But the mind of Elizabeth Barrett was lively and secular and satirical. Books were to her not an end in themselves but a substitute for living.

She wrote because she was an invalid and "forbidden to scamper on the grass." She pitted her intellect against Aeschylus and Plato because she was not permitted to argue about politics with living men and women. During her years as an isolated invalid, before she managed to break free from from the clutches of her domineering father and escape into the real world with the poet Browning, "she had lived shut off, guessing at what was outside, and inevitably magnifying what was within." By the time she escaped it was too late. She was dazzled when she was at last able to meet "face to face and without mask the Humanity of the age and speak the truth of it out plainly." She was also too weak. As a result she was incapable of ordinary response: "she saw and felt so much that she did not altogether know what she felt or what she saw." Inevitably *Aurora Leigh* suffered as a result. Virginia Woolf implies that many of the Victorian women who so enjoyed this work found themselves similarly isolated from the outside world, and as such incapable of any realistic or appropriate poetic response to it.

Likewise, it is not difficult to see the autobiographical element in Virginia Woolf's response to *Aurora Leigh* and its author. In her creative work, one of Virginia's main aims was to render the verisimilitude of consciousness, the truth of her own experiences. Such "truth" was constantly threatened by the distortions, exaggerations, and even delusions of her mental illness. She too spent long periods in solitude and worried deeply about her isolation from the world of "appropriate response." Her unforgiving analysis of Elizabeth Barrett Browning was paralleled by a similar self-analysis.

In a book devoted to essays on her reactions to other writers, Virginia Woolf impishly ends with an essay entitled "How Should One Read a Book?" Her answer to this question is indicative of her ideas far beyond literature: "The only advice, indeed, that one person can give another about reading is to take no advice, to follow your own instincts, to use your own reason, to come to your own conclusions." Little wonder that Margery Fry had been shocked by Virginia's ideas during their tour of Greece together; this was hardly the kind of advice that would have appealed to the principal of a ladies' college at Cambridge. Such advice also irritated the young, up-and-coming Cambridge literary critic F. R.

Leavis, who now saw Virginia and her friends as very much the establishment, whose views were to be pilloried. Leavis believed that literature needed to be freed from the attentions of the sophisticated Bloomsbury clique and their ilk in metropolitan London. But it is difficult to pillory the liberal advice of Virginia Woolf, except by attempting to impose one's own views and interpretations. So her modernistic prose-poetry and challenging attempts to convey human consciousness were rejected in favor of the forthright prose-poetry of D. H. Lawrence and his full-blooded pronouncements of what life was about. Leavis's new creed stressed moral purpose rather than creative freedom.

Having been the progressive young modernist, Virginia Woolf now found herself viewed as an obstacle to the true progress of the novel. F. R. Leavis launched his authoritative critical magazine *Scrutiny* in 1932, with the avowed aim of restoring "authenticity" to literature, insisting upon "moral seriousness" and "concrete realism" in the modern novel. Over the following decades *Scrutiny* would damage Virginia Woolf's reputation, with Leavis's influence holding sway well beyond Cambridge. Although Virginia was far from being eclipsed, she would not receive her due. Not until the rise of feminism and the recognition of the power of her ideas—in both fiction and nonfiction—would she be restored to her rightful place in the pantheon of modern British writers. Ironically, it is now D. H. Lawrence who appears to be lacking in some essential quality of literary truth. (Virginia Woolf was perceptive enough to recognize that he possessed the requisite "man-womanly" quality—though Lawrence himself found his female side, the homosexual element within his nature, all but impossible to live with.)

Virginia Woolf now embarked upon another novel. In contrast to her earlier creative works, her aim this time would be "factual" rather than "poetic." *The Years*, as this work came to be called, described in a series of episodes the life of a family from 1880 to the present day. In her own words: "It is to be an Essay-Novel . . . and it's to take in everything, sex, education, life, etc." The writing of this work would cause her

VIRGINIA WOOLF IN 90 MINUTES

immense trouble, involving many rewrites,
mostly in her attempts to resolve to problems
presented by an "essay-novel." How was the fiction to illustrate the ideas it embodied, yet at the
same time retain its vitality, have a convincing
life of its own? The problem was never fully resolved before *The Years* was published in 1937.
Even her loyal husband Leonard regarded it as a
"dead" novel; the public thought otherwise, and
The Years sold more copies on publication—in
Britain as well as America—than any of her previous works. However, consequent judgment has
tended to side with her husband. *The Years* is in
many ways Virginia Woolf's most traditional
novel, and as such seems devoid of the inspirational spark of her previous works:

> She was left alone. She was glad to be alone.
> She had no wish to talk. But next moment
> somebody stood beside her. It was Martin.
> He sat down beside her. She changed her at-
> titude completely.
>
> "Hullo, Martin!" she greeted him cordially.

Sadly, there are too many passages like this.

Three years earlier, Roger Fry had died. After the death of Lytton Strachey, Virginia had made long-term plans to write his biography, but these were now set aside to write a biography of Fry. Once again she appeared to be burying her talent in the "factual." (One has only to contrast this with her lyrical biography of the mythical beloved "Orlando.")

Many reasons have been suggested for this retreat. Virginia Woolf was now in her forties, an age when the lyrical impulse is often in abeyance. Another, more pressing reason, may be seen in her constant (and growing) fear of madness. There is no doubt that the exercise of her poetic talent was often disturbing to her mental equilibrium. Last, but by no means least, was the worsening political situation. Hitler's Germany was now menacing the whole of Europe. When the Nazis invaded Poland in 1939, Britain and France declared war: the Second World War had begun. In 1940 the Nazis invaded France, quickly overrunning it, and a German invasion of Britain seemed imminent. The Blitz began in London, and the Woolfs' London house was bombed. They retired to their home at Rodwell in Kent, only a short distance from the sea. Across the water the Germans were preparing to invade. Nazi policy with regard to Jews was well known, and Virginia became increasingly fearful about the fate of Leonard, who had so often been her only support in times of need. She also knew of the Nazis' policy toward the mentally ill. If the threatened invasion took place, they might both end up in concentration camps.

In an attempt to divert herself from her growing concerns, Virginia embarked upon a new novel, *Between the Acts*. It was in many ways an attempt to reconcile her factual vision of "the dialectics of history" with her poetic vision of beauty. It describes the events of a summer's day in a country house, where a historical pageant is enacted, all of which is ominously overshadowed by the coming of war. The book is filled with a complex interweaving of poetic and conceptual themes, all conveyed with arresting and resonant imagery—as in this scene where the players in the pageant dance:

The gramophone blared. Dukes, priests, shepherds, pilgrims and serving men took hands and danced. The idiot scampered in and out. Hands joined, heads knocking, they danced around the majestic figure of Mrs. Clark, licensed to sell tobacco, on her soap box.

We can see the scene in both its commonplace and its poetic aspect—yielding some profound imagistic thought. But the effort of all this proved too much for its author. When she had finished *Between the Acts* there was nothing further to distract her. Depressed beyond measure, fearful for her future and her own sanity, Virginia Woolf drowned herself in the nearby River Ouse on March 28, 1941.

Date Due Slip

Harris County Public Library
HCPL Atascocita
02/21/11   04:44PM

****

PATRON: OKEZIE BRIDGETT A

DUE DATE: 03/07/11
CALL NO. B Depp
ITEM: 34028066706152
  Johnny Depp : a biography /

Please Keep Slip With Book

Afterword

Virginia Woolf's final letter to her husband spoke of the "complete happiness" he had given her, and how "No one could have done more than you have done." This was a kindness—in contravention of her Bloomsbury code of frankness, of openness. It was in many ways an ultimate admission of despair. She no longer had the energy to explain, or even try to explain, what she felt. Leonard was the person to whom she was closest, yet even to him she could not explain her essential bewilderment and frustration. She could not make him see what she felt. In the midst of their mutual devotion was a colossal misunderstanding. A large part of this was the misundersanding that will always exist between the sane and the mentally troubled. It is all but impossible for even the most imaginative understanding to cross this line. Leonard tried to be deeply understanding but could not make such an imaginative leap (for all his efforts). Another large part of this misunderstanding was the failure, yet again, of a male and a female mind to meet on equal grounds. In such a male-oriented society, this was all but impossible. Virginia Woolf could not explain the full force of what ailed her, let alone her needs as a woman, the fears, the unfulfillment: the impossibility of being herself. Leonard wished to explain to her that her fears were groundless, that the bewildering chimeras summoned up by her disturbed mind could be banished by rest, understanding, and reason. Alas, such male rationality proved an inadequate response to her troubled female sensibility.

Joyce, Pound, Eliot, Woolf . . . Virginia Woolf would take her place among the finest English-language modernists of the early twentieth century. Of these, Joyce has now emerged as transcendent. Over the coming years, Pound would suffer for his fascist ideas, Eliot has suffered on account of his religiosity, and Virginia Woolf on account of her insistently female point of view. But later this very element would come to be seen as her lasting strength and originality. In her lifetime, D. H. Lawrence had been championed on account of his "natural maleness"— whereas Virginia Woolf's "natural femaleness" had been held against her. The position is now reversed. It is Lawrence whose sexual attitudes and pontifications on the natural behavior of mankind seem dated, muddled, and inappropriate. On the other hand, Virginia Woolf's ideas in her essays, novels, and "biography" (*Orlando*) continue to inform and inspire those who seek to resolve, or simply investigate, the ever-present question of gender and compatibility. *A Room of One's Own* discusses problems that remain alive today. This shift of emphasis and relevance has its parallels in the reputations of her contemporaries. The bravura bohemian painter Augustus John was considered by many (especially in Britain) to be a major artist in his lifetime, while the quieter talent of his sister Gwen John

109

remained neglected in a Parisian garret. Augustus John himself was well aware of the injustice of this, remarking to his disbelieving friends that one day he would be remembered merely as the brother of Gwen. Such is coming to be the case. More pertinent and revealing is the case of the celebrated French existentialist philosopher Jean-Paul Sartre, whose work completely outshone that of his partner Simone de Beauvoir during their lifetimes. Nowadays it is Sartre's modish Marxist existentialism that has fallen into neglect, while the feminist ideas put forward by de Beauvoir in her pioneering *The Second Sex* and other texts on feeling and grieving are seen as fundamental to present preoccupations. This is de Beauvoir's verdict on Virginia Woolf and the way forward:

> . . . we can count on the fingers of one hand the women who have traversed the given in search of its secret dimensions: Emily Brontë has questioned death, Virginia Woolf life. . . . Art, literature, philosophy are attempts to found the world anew on a human liberty:

that of the individual creator; to entertain such pretension one must first unequivocally assume the status of a being who has liberty . . . one must first emerge from [the world] into a sovereign solitude if one wants to try to regain a grasp upon it

The central message of *A Room of One's Own* remains true to each ensuing generation.

Virginia Woolf's Chief Works

The Voyage Out (1915)[†]
Night and Day (1919)[†]
Jacob's Room (1922)[†]
The Common Reader (first series) (1925)[†]
Mrs. Dalloway (1925)[*][†]
To the Lighthouse (1927)[*][†]
Orlando (1928)[*][†]
A Room of One's Own (1929)[*][†]
The Waves (1931)[*][†]
The Common Reader (second series) (1932)[†]
The Years (1937)[†]
Roger Fry: A Biography (1940)
Between the Acts (1941)[*][†]

[*]major works
[†]discussed in text

Chronology of
Virginia Woolf's Life and Times

1882   January 25, Virginia Woolf born Virginia
        Stephen, third child of Leslie and Julia
        Stephen, at Kensington in London.

1890   About this time, sexually molested by her
        eighteen-year-old half-brother Gerald.

1895   Death of Virginia's mother, Julia, in May.
        Suffers serious mental breakdown
        throughout summer.

1904   Possible sexual advances by her older half-
        brother George. Death of Virginia's father,
        Sir Leslie Stephen in May. Suffers another
        serious mental breakdown throughout
        summer, during which she attempts suicide
        by throwing herself from a window.

Virginia and remaining Stephen family children all move to 46 Gordon Square in Bloomsbury. Virginia writes anonymous literary reviews for *Times*.

1905   Family trip to Greece, after which Virginia's brother Thoby dies of typhoid in London.

1910   Together with brother Adrian and his Cambridge friends, takes part in *Dreadnought* hoax.

1911   Virginia marries Leonard Woolf. Ensuing long period of mental illness, including a suicide attempt.

1914   Outbreak of First World War.

1915   Virginia Woolf publishes her first novel, *The Voyage Out*.

1917   Lenin leads Bolshevik Revolution in Russia.

1918   End of First World War.

1919   Virginia Woolf publishes *Night and Day*.

1922   *Annus mirabilis* of modernism: Joyce publishes *Ulysses* in Paris after its rejection by the Hogarth Press. First appearance of T. S. Eliot's *The Waste Land*, which is published by the Hogarth Press the following year. Virginia Woolf publishes *Jacob's Room*.

1925   Virginia Woolf publishes her novel *Mrs. Dalloway* as well as her first collection of essays, *The Common Reader*.

1926   Britain paralyzed by general strike.

1927   Virginia Woolf publishes *To the Lighthouse*.

1929   Wall Street crash signals worldwide Great Depression. Virginia Woolf publishes *A Room of One's Own*.

1931   Publishes *The Waves*.

1932   Publishes *The Common Reader* (second series).

1933   Hitler comes to power in Germany.

1937   Virginia Woolf publishes *The Years*.

1939   Nazi Germany invades Poland, initiating of Second World War in Europe.

1940   Virginia Woolf writes *Roger Fry: A Biography*.

1941   Completes *Between the Acts*. March: depression and fear of madness cause her to commit suicide by drowing in River Ouse.

117

Recommended Reading

Quentin Bell, *Virginia Woolf: A Biography* (Harvest Books, 1974). The first biography, also by a fellow member of the Bloomsbury Group who knew her well. This is still regarded by many as the standard work. But in the manner of the period, it does not examine certain matters in the intimate detail that later readers have come to expect.

Rachel Bowlby, ed., *Virginia Woolf* (Longman, 1992). A series of perceptive critical essays on various aspects of Virginia Woolf's life, work, and feminism. These cover aspects of literature, structuralism, and psychology. They provide a useful introduction to these fields in relation to Woolf's work, indicating where one can follow up these interests.

Hermione Lee, *Virginia Woolf* (Vintage, 1999). An excellent full-scale biography which in more than eight hundred pages manages to deal with most of the voluminous material available about Virginia Woolf, her life, and Bloomsbury times. Also contains much shrewd analysis of Virginia without making this intrusive.

John Lehmann, *Virginia Woolf* (Thames and Hudson, 1999). A shorter biography of Virginia by a surviving fellow member of the Bloomsbury Group who knew her well. Lavishly illustrated with many photos, drawings, papers, and paintings related to Virginia and the Group. These succeed in capturing the atmosphere of their lives as well as any words.

Nigel Nicolson and Joanne Trautmann Banks, eds., *The Collected Letters of Virginia Woolf* (Hogarth Press, 1980). These six volumes reveal Virginia Woolf in all her moods. They contain much catty gossip which circulated in the Bloomsbury Group as well as many telling details from her everyday life. For those who haven't the time or inclination to plow through the entire collection, there is an excellent *Selected Letters* edited by Joanne Trautmann Banks.

RECOMMENDED READING

Susan Roe, *Writing and Gender: Virginia Woolf's Writing Practice* (Palgrave Macmillan, 1991). A short but insightful examination of Woolf's major literary works with reference to a variety of topics, including sexual politics, and especially her writing practice, with many illuminating insights into her intentions and revisions.

Virginia Woolf, *Moments of Being*, edited by Jeanne Schulkind (Harvest Books, 1985). Posthumously collected pieces of autobiographical writing, some parts of which are highly revelatory. "A Sketch of the Past" contains the description of, and feelings about, the notorious incident with her half-brother Gerald. "Am I a Snob?" gives a good indication of that class-ridden British era.

Virginia Woolf, *A Writer's Diary* (Harvest Books, 2003). Another posthumously published work containing extracts selected by her husband, Leonard Woolf, from the diary she kept from 1915 to her death twenty-six years later. This offers an excellent insight into her feelings and ideas as well as the way she saw herself as a writer. A full five-volume edition, edited by Anne Olivier Bell, is also available.

Index

A NOTE ON THE AUTHOR

Paul Strathern has lectured in philosophy and mathematics and now lives and writes in London. He is the author of the enormously successful series Philosophers in 90 Minutes. A Somerset Maugham Prize winner, he is also the author of books on history and travel, as well as five novels. His articles have appeared in a great many publications, including the *Observer* (London) and the *Irish Times*.

Paul Strathern's 90 Minutes series in philosophy, also published by Ivan R. Dee, includes individual books on Thomas Aquinas, Aristotle, St. Augustine, Berkeley, Confucius, Derrida, Descartes, Dewey, Foucault, Hegel, Heidegger, Hume, Kant, Kierkegaard, Leibniz, Locke, Machiavelli, Marx, J. S. Mill, Nietzsche, Plato, Rousseau, Bertrand Russell, Sartre, Schopenhauer, Socrates, Spinoza, and Wittgenstein.